PRESTON BAILEY FLOWERS

Text **ANNETTA HANNA**

Photographs **JOHN LABBE**

RIZZOLI
NEW YORK

INTRODUCTION

Every day that I work, I am surrounded by flowers, and I must ask myself: how can I make these flowers more beautiful? As a floral designer and event planner, this is supposed to be part of my job, after all. But the best answer I can come up with is, I can't! There is no way I can improve upon something that is already perfect. After working for so many years with flowers, I remain continually humbled by them. The only solution I have found to the dilemma posed by my work is simply to offer my own interpretations of what Mother Nature so lavishly displays. If I am lucky, I may then be able to inspire in others some of the awe and pleasure I feel every time I pick a flower. And it is those feelings of awe and pleasure that led me to write *Flowers*. Let me be clear: although I have included tips and insights into the process of floral design, this is no step-by-step, do-it-yourself guide to flower arranging. Many of the events featured here required the assistance of a skilled team of artisans. But I believe that the more we are exposed to the beauty of flowers, the more we can find ways to add that beauty to our own lives, whether with the help of a florist or with a nice vase and a simple grouping of flowers.

In any event, experiencing anew the pleasure of flowers is the goal. This can happen when you walk into a grand room filled with the most beautiful displays of flowers, but it can also happen when you sit down at a table to find a perfect little orchid tucked into your napkin. I like to layer such moments of delight throughout an event, so that each segment has a unique appeal. For example, a wedding may feature one palette of colors and flowers for the ceremony and a contrasting look for the reception or dinner.

The scale of arrangements creates another type of rhythm for an event, with tall displays grabbing attention and smaller pieces unfolding their charms as the evening progresses. As an ideal complement to flowers, I like to add lighting elements, whether with cutting-edge technology or with classic candles—who doesn't look great by candlelight! Lately I have also been incorporating crystals into my design planning, and I find them to be a wonderful way to add even more ambiance to an event. I love the interplay between the bright radiance of crystals and the soft glow of flowers. And there's nothing like a cascade of faceted crystals to reflect and multiply the colors of a floral display.

The colors of flowers are, for me, strongly linked to various emotions and sensations: pinks, fuchsias, and lavenders suggest feminine beauty; blues, greens, and turquoises evoke harmony; reds, oranges, and bright yellows promise change and festivity; and cream and white convey a sense of elegance. Of course, we all have different responses to colors, which is why I always start a project by asking my clients which are their favorites and which they dislike. Whatever the palette becomes for a particular event, as a professional designer I don't follow hard and fast rules for using color, since I don't really have any: I will happily contrast or harmonize colors, make them pop or make them whisper. A final design reflects the nature of the event, not the dictates of a style book. (I will admit, though, to a personal love for the warmer end of the color spectrum, which probably reflects my childhood spent exploring the tropical landscape of Panama.)

After color, shape is most influential in determining the impact of a floral design. Clients often have definite preferences when it comes to shape; they may gravitate toward loose, asymmetrical, and organic displays, or they may instead ask for structured, symmetrical, and classical arrangements. I am drawn to the shapes of trees and find them to be one of the most effective ways to bring nature indoors, particularly when designing for a large space. I am especially fond of graceful canopies of branches, and I find myself returning to that image in many of my designs. I have woven together branches and flowers to recreate these arches, but I've also used ribbons and crystals to do so. And, of course, the floral sculptures that have become one of my trademark designs are all about shape. Using blossoms in three-dimensional creations, in the same way a sculptor might use clay, is one way to expand upon the pleasure of working with flowers. When those sculptures are of birds or fish or elegant poodles—well, that's my idea of a Garden of Eden, with flora and fauna combined.

And so once again, I return to the notion of finding pleasure in using flowers. Each story in this book represents an adventure in my ongoing attempt to work with perfection. I invite you to find your own pleasure in *Flowers*.

"Regardless of its size or complexity, the perfect floral arrangement is the one that makes you stop for an instant and smile with surprise and delight."

AN ALL-WHITE WEDDING IN A TROPICAL PARADISE

There are places in the world that are almost overwhelmingly beautiful, and the tropical Indonesian island of Java is one example of this near-perfection. When I was asked to design the floral landscape for a wedding to be held in one of Java's loveliest homes, I knew that my challenge would lie in creating bold arrangements to complement this dazzling setting. My gorgeous client had a very clear vision of what she wanted: an all-white wedding, with the garden transformed into an elegant, open-air dining area filled with lush cascades of flowers and classically appointed tables. More than a thousand guests would be transported along a series of winding roads and would enter the magnificent house before moving outdoors for a seated dinner. To welcome my client's guests, we began with the estate's handsome entrance gates, bedecking the scrolled metalwork with garlands of hydrangeas and white roses; more hydrangeas, massed in abundance, entirely covered a ring of boxwoods that circled the lily-filled pond. I decided to break one of my prime rules of outdoor entertaining—always use a dining tent!—and Mother Nature smiled upon us: it turned out to be a glorious night. Strands of tiny white lights twinkled like stars in the clear sky above the checkerboard dance floor of black and white tiles; the only touch of color at the tables came from the amber glow of low tea lights and tall, slim tapers set in silver candlesticks. Small white orchids, strung along invisible wires and swaying with the graceful movement of willow trees, covered the panels and sculptures that framed the space. I love adding unexpected touches of humor in my designs, so we plaited white roses into a soft necklace for the stern stone lion that lives in the estate's garden. And for more magic, the light-trimmed carousel, with its flower-covered horses and carriages, actually worked, offering rides to the delighted guests. The exquisite home is filled with remarkable works of art, rich materials, and saturated hues, and my client's brilliant choice of an all-white floral palette resulted in classic arrangements that were amplified by the setting. Thanks to my client, I discovered one of the island's most extraordinary craft traditions: skilled artisans weave together masses of fresh jasmine flowers to create a crochetlike "fabric" that makes amazing table runners. Java is truly a miracle of nature enhanced by design.

"An extraordinary setting in the hills of Java inspired the floral design for an all-white wedding layered with elegance and delight."

PAGES 10–11: The handsome gates swung open to welcome more than a thousand guests to a magical setting. ABOVE AND RIGHT: I admired the lyrical metal curves of the gates and tried to capture their wonderful sense of movement with garlands of hydrangeas, white roses, and white snapdragons. PAGES 14–15: We used masses of white hydrangeas to entirely cover the ring of boxwood that surrounded the lily-filled pond.

PAGES 16–17: A grand portico led to the dining area, which was open to the warm night. PAGES 18–19: Black and white checkerboard tiles accented the all-white design. ABOVE AND RIGHT: I used the tall floral arrangements to create an overall rhythm for the space, but since guests typically spend much of their evening seated at the table, I wanted the lower, eye-level arrangements to be as engaging as a great dinner companion. PAGES 22–23: A lacy grid of little white lights formed a fine veil overhead, adding a sense of intimacy to the dining area.

LEFT AND ABOVE: We flanked the entrance to the dining area with panels of wisteria and phalaenopsis orchids. More garlands of white roses and white hydrangeas wound around the topiaries and even embellished a fierce stone garden lion. PAGES 26–27: My beautiful client loves merry-go-rounds, and we were more than happy to create a very special treat for her guests—a flower-covered carousel that actually worked.

PAGES 28–29: With its grand rooms this remarkable home offered us many settings that were perfect for large arrangements. ABOVE AND RIGHT: Delicate strands of jasmine were strung like pearl necklaces around the elegant silver candelabras and garnished the low bowls of white roses, white hydrangeas, and white phalaenopsis that lined the tables. PAGES 32–32: Because I love to add local elements to grand events, I was thrilled to find a group of artisans in Java who could weave together flowers to create these absolutely amazing floral table runners.

LEFT AND ABOVE: It was a delight to use the owners' lovely art objects for our arrangements including this classic silver tureen. PAGES 36–37: One of the great challenges when working in an extraordinary setting is to find the right balance between not enough and too much. Flower arrangements must be bold enough to capture the guests' attention, but they should never try to compete with an already sublime setting. Using a pared-down color palette allows you to create lavish displays that can complement and enhance even the most magnificent space.

PAGES 40–41: Lilacs, wisteria, clematis, jasmine, and hydrangeas formed a canopy for the wedding's gazebo. PAGES 42–43: We used soft pink, ivory and white blossoms in our arrangements, accenting this palette with flashes of deeper color that we added to the garden. PAGES 44–45: I love to sculpt with flowers, so we built a three-tiered stand covered with dusty miller leaves, roses, hydrangeas, tulips, lilacs, sweet pea, peonies, and orchids to hold the dinner's escort cards. LEFT AND ABOVE: Roses, hydrangeas, jasmine, and peonies were loosely arranged in old-fashioned ceramic pitchers. PAGES 48–49: Dusky mauve roses were casually set on crisp white napkins to relax the formality of a classically set table.

ABOVE AND RIGHT: Nothing is more delicately romantic than a bouquet filled with hydrangeas, peonies, sweet peas, and helleborus. A garland of blossoms dressed the bride's faithful friend, who was an important part of the wedding party. PAGES 52–53: The polished wooden walkway offered a petal-edged path through our enchanted garden. PAGES 54–55: We covered one of the main walls of the house with a climbing display of hydrangeas and boxwood that glowed at nightfall with a myriad of tiny lights, adding a sense of magic to the evening.

PAGES 58–59: The gazebo's canopy seemed to capture light from the sky above. ABOVE AND RIGHT: We used clear glass beads to create rounded containers for the dinner arrangements of roses, cymbidium orchids, hydrangeas, and lisianthus. PAGES 62–63: The roses in the bride's bouquet were complemented by white nerine and tiny crystals. Glass vases held roses, hydrangeas, agapanthus, and dendrobium orchids, accented by clear crystals. PAGES 64–65: Falling from the canopy's crown was a curtain of orchids and crystals woven together in light-filled strands.

FLOWERS FOR A MOST ELEGANT BRIDE

Ask me to describe an elegant wedding, and many gorgeous images come to my mind. But ask me to describe the epitome of an elegant bride, and I would have to reply with one name: Ivanka Trump. Helping her plan her wedding was a rare pleasure for me, as time and time again Ivanka revealed her impeccable taste and classic design sense. The ceremony, held at the Trump National Golf Club in Bedminster, New Jersey, took place in an all-white tent with walls of windows that offered panoramic views of the rich fall foliage and distant rolling hills. Gauzy white curtains flanked the entrance and framed an aisle canopied by hand-woven green branches and white dendrobium orchids. The chuppah was trimmed with a selection of roses and hydrangeas, like a vision of spring in bloom set against the russet backdrop of autumn. After the ceremony, the cocktail reception featured a palette of vibrant reds and greens; roses, dahlias, bells of Ireland, hand-sewn garlands of petals, and glossy magnolia leaves filled tall containers and wrapped a graceful balustrade. As the guests approached the dining area, they were greeted by an escort table that showcased a sumptuous arrangement of roses, with lily of the valley and tassels of green amaranthus; to counterpoint this lavish display, we placed tiny glass vases alongside the escort cards, each one holding a pure white gardenia for the guests to add to a lapel or tuck into the ribbons of an evening bag. We created a medley of arrangements for the dinner tables, unified by the all-white palette but varied in height and accented by candles ranging in size from tapers to pillars. The tallest arrangements, poised atop crystal holders that provided height without obscuring sight lines, incorporated pillar candles and strands of crystals within their crowns of gardenias and roses. Smaller arrangements were set in stone-finished vases that added texture to the refined tabletops; more pillar candles were simply circled by tiny tea roses. To surprise and delight the guests, we placed clear Plexiglas "moats" down the center of some of the tables; these held pillar candles and posies of lily of the valley, lisianthus, and ranunculus, as well as single gardenias that floated freely in the clear water. I happily admit that my approach to arranging flowers tends toward options that are offered by color and drama, but working with my lovely Ivanka reminded me of all the excitement to be found in a classic design, one befitting this most elegant of brides.

"A sophisticated bride with a refined sense of style reminded me of the power of classic floral arrangements to generate a wealth of visual excitement."

PAGES 76–77: At the entrance to the dinner, the escort table offered a fragrant welcome of white gardenias. ABOVE AND RIGHT: It can be great fun to work with different types of containers: texture, height, placement, and shape can all be varied to add elements of intrigue and surprise to a party. Upon entering a space, the eye is first drawn to the tallest arrangements; at the table, lower arrangements allow for new discoveries over the course of the dinner. PAGES 80–81: A Plexiglas "moat" held candles and small bouquets of flowers, with gardenias floating in the water.

PAGES 84–85: Entrances, whether in a private home or a public venue, can easily set the tone for everything to come, so a hallway console or escort table is the ideal spot for a breathtakingly gorgeous arrangement: this is the place to pull out all the stops and make the night unforgettable. ABOVE AND RIGHT: A variety of bold red blossoms created a neatly formed topiary. I like to place conversation starters at the entry to a dinner, so that arriving guests are encouraged to strike up discussions on, for example, the magic that seems to hold a bouquet suspended in thin air.

LEFT AND ABOVE: Color is such a direct way to convey emotion, with red carrying an unmistakable message of fun and festivity. Containers can be slender and minimal or big and bold, but they must never interfere with the flow of conversation. PAGES 90–91: Lined up like a row of curvy showgirls, our big fabric vases held flamboyant arrangements of amaryllis, roses, hypericums, and orchids that seemed ready to kick off a great party.

PAGES 94–95: A frame was suspended from the room's high ceiling and covered with a dense canopy of purple wisteria, lilacs, and crystals. PAGES 96–97: Held the night before the gala, a smaller dinner in a more modern space featured a different color story of pink, red, and lavender miniature roses, hydrangeas, and cattleya and dendrobium orchids; the containers were sculpted using flowers to create architecturally inspired arrangements that related to the main event's classic setting. PAGES 98–99: Light reflected off the flowers and cast a lavender glow.

PAGES 102–103: The arched entrance to the wedding pavilion was animated by lights and crystals—a spectacular introduction to the night to come. PAGES 104–105: The pavilion's interior called for a seamless integration of technology, craft, and creative problem-solving. The dance floor contained LED lights, with clear panels placed above countless crystals and pink hydrangeas to create a patterned surface. RIGHT AND ABOVE: Bathed in a swirl of colored lights, the dining area was punctuated by crystal canopies crowned with tall tapers. PAGES 108–109: The royal family's table was highlighted by another three-dimensional archway of crystals and enhanced with an intricate crystal crest.

PAGES 112–113: We built a lavishly gilded mirror for the seating area at the entrance to the party. PAGES 114–115: A stationary carousel added whimsy to the space. PAGES 116–117: Colorfully bedecked in flowers and crystals, each horse held a clear cocktail table. PAGES 118–119: The evening's arrangements contained orchids, roses, agapanthus, eremurus, and birds of paradise. It is always a bit tricky to work with such boldly colored flowers—the payoff comes when the display "pops." LEFT AND ABOVE: We built an ornate ceiling panel to create more intimacy in the vast space and to serve as a surface for colored lights. PAGES 122–123: The silver trays upon which the vases stood not only mirrored the flowers but also added a few inches of height to the large arrangements, raising them above the diners' sight lines.

121

PAGES 126–127: With its aisle of sparkling trees, the wedding ceremony was the start of an evening filled with shimmering crystals. PAGES 128–129: Guests were welcomed by a grand arch of roses, lisianthus, orchids, stocks, freesias, and hydrangeas, which led directly to a flower-crowned sculpture that glistened like spun sugar at the center of the escort table. ABOVE AND LEFT: Clear crystals accented the lavish array of flowers that filled tall vases at each table, while one of the tiered dessert stands showcased colored stones, phalaenopsis orchids, hydrangeas, and roses.

PAGES 132–133: My lovely client and I had a marvelous time working together, knowing that expectations would be sky-high for this once-in-a-lifetime party. We created special showpieces that reflected the bride's affinity for all things Russian, including an opulent samovar and two flowered bears that became immortalized in countless photographs taken by the guests. PAGES 134–135: A tornado of butterflies rose skyward from a dessert table. LEFT AND ABOVE: Gift tables left the departing guests with lingering visions of orchids, roses, handmade petal garlands, and crystals. PAGES 138–139: The dining area was encircled by projected images and was filled with layers of lights.

PAGES 142–143: The wedding tent provided a clean, modern backdrop for our trees crowned by branches of silky apricot, peach, and ivory ribbons. PAGES 144–145: White orchids and handmade rose petal sculptures were woven into the ribbons for an added surprise. I loved how the canopies swayed and shimmered in the tent's gauzy white light. LEFT AND ABOVE: The cocktail reception was punctuated by tall arrangements of orchids, dogwood branches, and horsetails that seemed to erupt from nearly invisible Plexiglas containers. Standing panels of Plexiglas repeated the decorative cut-out shapes used in the floral containers and provided dramatic framework for the space.

PAGES 148–149: My clients had originally asked for a blue and white floral palette, but since there are so few blue flowers in nature, we decided instead to use a profusion of white flowers set against the dinner tent's deep blue backdrop. ABOVE AND RIGHT: Using glass balls and fiber-optic technology, we built chandeliers that seemed to float in mid-air. We attached blossoms to invisible wires and suspended them inside waterless glass vases to add a touch of magic to the tall arrangements that graced some tables. PAGES 152–153: Tables varied in being decorated with either low or high arrangements, so the two types of settings had to be equally impressive: no one wants to be seated at a "lesser" table!

PAGE 156–157: We created our own blossoms, using a mix of tulips, carnations, and waxflowers. PAGE 158–159: A flamingo and a parrot were two of our floral flights of fancy. PAGES 160–161: To greet the guests, we suspended from invisible wires a sculpted swan in flight as a fanciful expression of the evening's avian theme. LEFT AND ABOVE: The glass-walled tent permitted views of Central Park, a perfect backdrop for hot pink table settings. Scarlet faux macaws injected splashes of bright blue, green, and yellow, making the flamingo decals that we added to glass vases appear almost sedate in contrast. PAGE 164–165: Lush arrangements popped with tropical colors against the park's rich green foliage.

PAGES 168–169: For one event featuring a palette of warm yellows and oranges, our designs included tulips, calla lilies, snap dragons, forsythia, gloriosas, and orchids set in a classical silver urn that we placed on a pedestal covered with miniature mums and decorated with jewellike petal ornaments. PAGES 170–171: A most delicate and challenging presentation entailed making soup bowls from real ostrich eggs, each topped by a pearl finial. For a far less nerve-racking design, we decorated dinner napkins with orchids and rose petals, Gerbera daisies, and crystal baubles. ABOVE AND RIGHT: For a color scheme of purple, pink, and fuchsia, we built different types of tall containers containing orchids, hydrangeas, and wisteria. PAGES 174–175: Another presentation of the same flowers shifted the color scheme toward red, with a vase sculpted entirely of crimson dahlias.

PAGES 178–179: Although the ceremony was held in a sleek, contemporary space, the reception took place in what had once been one of New York's grandest banks. PAGES 180–181: We built the chandeliers and the proscenium, and swathed the space with fabric that was washed with a warm ruby light. ABOVE AND RIGHT: Profusions of orchids and calla lilies exploded from tall vases that were sculpted using dahlias. PAGES 184–185: As soon as the couple was pronounced married, we transformed the room by changing the lights from a cool blue to an exuberant rose, by projecting images of trees and flowers in full bloom, accentuating the message of new life and new beginnings.

A PICTURE OF LOVELINESS

Unveiled after weeks or months of intense planning, building, and fine-tuning, my "products" have a lifespan that can be measured in hours. Almost before we begin setting up, the event is over; the designs live on only in photographs and memories. I know that the ephemeral nature of flowers is part of their beauty, but it does seem a shame to break down all those arrangements when the guests depart. This is one reason I love designing exhibitions that can last for several days and that are open to the public. One such floral display was produced for New York City's Bridal Week in conjunction with The Knot, an online wedding planning site. Our location: the soaring lobby of the New York Public Library's main branch on Fifth Avenue. Our star: a gorgeous fourteen-foot-tall bride bedecked in a glorious cascade of roses, phalaenopsis orchids, and hydrangeas. Our mannequin's flowing dress and headpiece of calla lilies sparkled with the same crystals that we used to accent her life-size canine companions. Stylishly clipped in white carnations and ivy leaves, the poodle groom sported a bow tie; his buxom but elegant bride struck a regal pose in her crystal circlet. We had so much fun with those pooches. Of course, longevity was a key factor in our flower choices. In my experience, roses are very durable, capable of lasting up to twenty-four hours without water. But to add extra hours to their freshness, we immersed the hydrangeas, roses, and carnations in hydrated floral foam; the orchids were inserted in floral water tubes. Brides are always the focus of attention—passersby stop to admire them everywhere in the world. But to my surprise, our mannequin attracted throngs of admirers, and lines of visitors patiently waited to have their picture taken with her. It truly was the beautiful bride's day.

"Longer-lived floral displays and sculptures for public exhibitions allow me to reach a broader audience, as witnessed by our traffic-stopping bride."

PRESTON BAILEY

Preston Bailey was born and raised in the tropical paradise of Panamá. Moving to New York City in 1968, he began his career in the design world as a fashion model at the age of 19. Ultimately, Preston's innate talent for design and dramatic sensibilities led him to the event industry. After 30 years in the business, Preston Bailey has become renowned for his gift for completely transforming raw, ordinary spaces into sumptuous, theatrical environments.

Because of Preston's unique ability to create breathtaking, memorable events, he has developed a client base that includes royalty, socialites, business moguls and celebrities such as Donald Trump, Oprah Winfrey, Joan Rivers, Donna Karan, Liza Minnelli, Laurence Fishburne, Bill Cosby, Matt Lauer, Michael Douglas and Catherine Zeta-Jones, Uma Thurman and Donny Deustch, among others.

Adding another dimension to his remarkable portfolio, Preston has been tapped for endorsements, launch events and licensing deals by major brands, including Sandals Resorts, Godiva, Hewlett-Packard, 1-800-Flowers, and more. His art installations have been commissioned to draw in consumers at prominent locations across the globe, such as London's Covent Garden and Hong Kong's fashionable Landmark Mall. In addition, he is the author of four best-selling books, "Design for Entertaining," "Fantasy Weddings," "Inspirations," and "Celebrations."

Preston recently partnered with The Wedding Planning Institute to offer a first-of-its-kind wedding and event planning course that is available at nearly 2,000 accredited colleges and universities in the United States. Preston is also much sought after both as a television guest and public speaker. His numerous national television appearances include *The Oprah Winfrey Show*, *Entertainment Tonight*, *Access Hollywood*, *Extra*, CBS's *The Early Show*, and NBC's *Today Show*. He regularly appears in dozens of publications including *Town & Country*, *Vogue*, *Vanity Fair*, *Elle Décor*, *The Wall Street Journal*, *The New York Times* and *New York Post*.

ACKNOWLEDGMENTS

This book of flowers would have never been possible without a loyal, dedicated, and persistent group of colleagues, clients, and friends.

I'd like to start by thanking my publisher Charles Miers, for allowing this book to come to life; my editor Kathleen Jayes, for her knowledge and perseverance; my designer Sam Shahid, for his ability to display my work on paper with such sophistication; and his colleague Jonathan Caplan, for his attention to detail. Thank you also to my very talented friend John Labbe, for taking great shots, mostly under great pressure; my friend Jill Cohen, for bringing this project to life, with her vast knowledge of the publishing world; my writer Annetta Hanna, for her ability to capture what's in my head better than I can say it.

On a more personal note, I'd like to thank my anchor and life partner Theo Bleckmann, for creating a centering place in my life.

Thank you to my beloved family: Aminta, Olivia, Belinda, Bernadette, Zellerita, Michael, Bernard, Beverly, Pearl, Clarence, for your loving support.

Marcy Blum, thank you for being my sounding board and loving friend.

My mentor Vicente Wolf, thank you for always having the right answer in difficult moments.

Erwin Gonzalez, for your humor and support.

My long time friend Mr. Bill Ash, for being a great listener.

To my supportive friends: Peter Azrak, Sylvia Weinstock, The Keidan family, The Novick family, Ayiri Oladunmoye in Nigeria, Litzia, MEK, Brenda Marsh, Reem Acra, Bershan Shaw, Andrea Blanch, Ritva, and Gloria Dare.

I'd like to thank my CEO Xoua Vang, for his brilliance in showing me how to grow my company; Anne Crenshaw, for her great ability in handling my finances; Sanaw Ledrod, you are without question the floral master of all times; my Business Administrator Rae, for always pointing me in the right direction; my friend and producer, Vivia Costalas, your integrity and work ethic have no boundaries.

My design team: Merv Garretson, Jee Sim, and Nikita Polansky.

My director of protocol Autumn Oser, Luis Fernando for your loyalty and Eduardo Martins, Cesar Ugarte, Michael Nolan, Oscar Simeon Jr. Iqbal Hayder, CarlosBelo Jr., Pedro Santos, Yessid Ortiz, Suwat Laorawat, Karell Roxas, Kesanee Ortiz, Anghakhana Chermsirivatana and Samorn Panpinyo.

My appreciation also goes to Donna Paitchel and David Schuster, for being great producers.

Thank you to all my most supportive clients: Biyan, Dani Soegiarso, Mr. & Mrs. Avner Copes, Mr. & Mrs. Bob Rich, Mr. & Mrs. Donald Trump, Mr. & Mrs. Jared Kushner, Mr. & Mrs. Joseph Krauetler (Levin), Mr. & Mrs. Peter Schafer (Anna Annisimova and husband), Mr. & Mrs. Suhas Daftuar, Mr. & Mrs. Lisjanto Tjiptobiantoro (Mr. & Mrs. Meity), Mr. Abel Arya (Carmel Groom), Mr. Arndt Oesterle, Mr. Vassili Anissimova, Mrs. Allison Stern (WCS), Mrs. Galina Anissimova, Ms. Carley Roney, Ms. Dale Brooks (WCS), Ms. Diane Jones (Finca), Ms. Karen Kwek, Ms. Soledad Gompf (Finca), Ms. Tania Tjiptobiantoro (Carmel Bride), Ms. Tiffany Reiser-Jacobson (WCS), Qatar Royal Family

A SPECIAL THANK YOU

Bali: Bali Catering: Benny Raj, Ngurah Tresna

Greece: Alexia Sideropoulou; Natasha Vlachopoulou; Thalia Exarchou

Indonesia: Ade Sari ADI Tent: Made, Wayan; Adjie; Alam Zaenuri; Alexander Ruiz; Alvin Soo; Anthony Pagano; ASP: Asep, Didi, Yusef; Bali Catering; Benny Raj; Brenda LaManna; Budi Hernowo; Dani Soegiarso; Danny Ceper; Davirex; Davy from Davirex; Didi Kusumanto; Dina Touwani; Duren; Erwin Gutawa Orchestra: Erwin Gutawa, Octaferry Ai, Novi Arvianty; Fio; Flora Lines: Dina, Elvina, Awien; Flow Design Firm:

Melina, Farid; FOCUS: Defry, Dion, Deny; Fumio Yasuda; Grucci: Donna Grucci-Butler, Phil Butler, Ian Mackenzie, Jane Engel, Jeffrey Engel, Michael Sullivan; Hamid; Inet Leimena; INFICO: Alit, Yuni; ISS: Indra, Paulus; Jimmy, Wira; Karen Kwek; Kim Hirst; Lily; Michael Curry Puppets: Michael Curry, Andrew Jagels, Nicholas Mahon, Elizabeth Robinson; Michael Nolan; Ngurah Tresna; No Limits: Doni, Dennis; PCP: Hendra, Pipin, Untung; Penta Wira: Bintang, Star; PT Bina Flora; Reka Citra: Budi, Toto; Rex Cokrowibowo; Robert D'Alessandro; Sebastian Ee; Sherwin Mahon; SIMA: Michael; Stupa Caspea: Eka, Harso, Yudi; Summit Productions: Donna Paitchel, David Shuster, Steve Paitchel; Tainted Love: Eddie Caipo, Douglas Carlson, Loy Wentworth, Steven Moon, Jeff Suburu, Jack Herndon, Clay Bell, Laura Secour, Doug Tel; Tasya; Theo Bleckmann; Tiara Josodirdjo; Toto Arto

Qatar: Aero Freight Services; Al Baddad Tents; Al Masara Al Daema; Alia Flowers from Bahrain; Al-Qadsia Furniture; Bernard Liberatore; Bin Yousef Cargo; Carsten Weiss; Daniel Jean; ECA2; Emma Juniper; Faisal Al Attiyah Trading & Contracting Est.; Fleuriot Fleurs; Ghazwan Makihe; Guillaume Duflot; Gulf Agency Qatar; Johanna Marsal; Julie Cugurno; Jun Balaba; L'Enclave; Melissa Weigel; Mr. Norman at Qatar Plant Hire; Mr. Shadi at Al Baddad Tents; Owen Marvel; Pablo Oliveira; Phaedra Dahdaleh; ProLuxon; Qatar Plant Hire; Qatar Radio & Television Corporation; Rabab Mahassen; Reka Citra; Richard Bellia; Rose Classic; Samir Said Faris; Saria Mahassen; Shadi Matouk; Simon Franklyn; Stephen Mar; Ted Davies at Qatar Plant Hire; Varghese Modiyil; Yousef Basel

Singapore: Alvin Soo; Floral procurement: Sebastian Ee

Taiwan: Carol Ng; Diva; Houchih Lin; Kai Pang; Kingsmen International; Selina Kao; Sophie Tsou; The Precious Moment; The Regent Taipei

United States: A + R Sewing; Alan M. Shukovsky; Alex Pogolny; Allen Burry; Arthur Bacall; Baked It Myself; Barbara Esses; Ben Moore; Bentley Meeker Lighting; Beta Iron Works; Better; Mousetrap; Bill Spinner; Blueprint Studios: Francisco Recabarren, Paul Moss; BMI-Blackbird Theatrical Services; Boutross Co. Inc.; Brenda LaManna; Brian Rieke; Brion Shemeley; Britt Adams; BZK-Ruth Fischl; Camille Chow; Catherine Whitworth; Cheryl Canter; Chris Dahlson; Classic Party Rentals; Crystal Studio; David Shapiro; Derek Widis; Designing Linens; Drape Kings; Elizabeth Lauriello; Ellen Weldon Designs; Erin Halley; Errin Verdesca; ESP, New York Inc; Floris Special Events; Frank Alexander NYC; Fred Marcus Photography; Frost Lighting; Fumio Yasuda; G. Page; Gary Merjian; Gio Draping; Gio Gonzalez; Gotham Hall; Great Performances; Guthrie DeBruyn; Harris Lane; Hartmann Studios: Matt Guelfi, Amber Salomon, Brad Jobin; Hi-Tech Events, LLC; IAC Buiding; Impact Lighting: Micky Fimbres; Ira Levy; Isabelle Buckley; Jamali Garden; James Munz; Jason Pulido; Jennifer Zabinski; Jerry Ragoobier; Jim Cotton; John Amedro; John Labbe; Johnny Smith; Julie Skarratt Photography, Inc.; Karl's Event Rentals; Kate McGarry; Keith Ganz; Keith Greco; Kelly Burns-Gaorin; L & M Lighting and Sound; L' Atelier; Lasting Art; La Tavola Linen: Deana Morrison; Lea Brumage; Leah Silberman; Levy Lighting; Liba Fabric Corp.; Linda Lieberman; Litsa Floris; Liz Kirschner; Marcy Blum; Marianne Bennet; Marisa Kuney; Mayesh Wholesale Florist, Inc.; Michael Nolan; Miller's Party Rentals; Mission Landscaping: Lee Stone, Rich Shaw; Moment Factory; Morris Azar; Norma Cohen; Nüage Designs, Inc; Okamoto Studio Design, Inc.; Olivier Cheng; Olivier Cheng Catering and Events; Party Rental Ltd.; Paula Leduc Catering: Paula Leduc, Tim Lilly; Paula Wellington; Paul Martinez; Philippe Cheng Photography; Planter Resource; Red Bliss Invitation Design; Rhona Graff; Robert Fountain; Royal Base Corporation; Russell Morin Fine Catering; Ruth Iacullo; Scharff Weisberg, Inc; Shawn King; Sherwin Mahon; Shintaro Okamoto; Showman Fabricators; Something Different Party Rental; St. Regis Hotel New York; Stamford Tent & Event Services; Stephen M. Frost; Steve Paitchel; Stratos Costalas; Summit Productions: Donna Paitchel, David Shuster; Sunny Kim; Susanne Jansson; Sylvia Weinstock Cakes; Tainted Love: Daniel Swan, Eddie Caipo, Douglas Carlson, Loy Wentworth, Steven Moon, Jeff Suburu, Jack Herndon, Clay Bell, Laura Secour, Doug T; Taylor Creative, Inc.; The Merion; The Pierre Hotel; Theo Bleckman; Tiffany New York; US Evergreen; Van Vliet, NY; Vowhouse; Waldorf Astoria, NYC; Wildflower Linen

PRESTON BAILEY ENTERTAINMENT & SET DESIGN, INC.

Michael Nolan
Florist

Robert (Merv) Garretson
Creative Director

Eduardo Martins
Operations Manager

Armi Roxas
Online Editor

Kesanee Ortiz
Floral Production Manager

Cesar Ugarte
Florist

Nikita Polyanksy
Designer

Xoua Vang
CEO

Anne Crenshaw
CFO

Vivia Costalas
Event Producer

Sanaw Ledrod
Director of Floral Design

Angkhana Chermsirivatana
Florist

Carlos Belo Jr.
Traffic Manager

Yessid Ortiz
Florist

Luiz Leite
Director of Operations

Jee Young Sim
Art Director

Pedro Santos
Production Assistant

Samorn Panpinyo
Florist

Autumn Oser
V.P. of Client Affairs

Suwat Laorawat
Florist

Iqbal Hayder
Director of Event Production

Oscar Simeon Jr.
Assistant Floral Manager

Raysheen Simpson
Business Administrator